The Story of Slavery

by

BOOKER T. WASHINGTON

ISBN: 978-1-63923-220-8

Printed: May 2022

Cover Art By: Amit Paul

Published and Distributed By:
Lushena Books
607 Country Club Drive, Unit E
Bensenville, IL 60106
www.lushenabooksinc.com/books

ISBN: 978-1-63923-220-8

The Story of Slavery

By Booker T. Washington
President of Tuskegee Institute; author of
"Up From Slavery," Etc.

With Biographical Sketch

Table of Contents

I...10
II 13
III 18
IV 23

BOOKER T. WASHINGTON BY EMMETT J. SCOTT

Booker T. Washington, the author of the following sketch of slavery in America, was himself born a slave, and the story of his life begins where "The Story of Slavery" leaves off. He was born about 1858 or 1859 on a plantation near Hales Ford, Va., about twenty-five miles east of the city of Roanoke, in a region which, now almost deserted, was in slavery days a flourishing tobacco country. A few years ago he was invited to speak at the annual fair at Roanoke, and took advantage of the opportunity to drive out to the old plantation to visit again the scene of his childhood. He met there several members of the Burroughs family to which he had formerly belonged, and with them he went through the old Burroughs house, which is standing, and talked over the old days.

It was while he was living there that he was awakened one morning to find his mother kneeling on the earth floor of the little cabin in which they lived, praying that "Lincoln and his armies might be successful and that one day she and her children might be free." It was here a little later on, as he tells us in the book, "Up From Slavery," in which he has related the story of his life, that he heard the announcement that he and all the other slaves were free.

"I recall," he says, "that some man who seemed to be a stranger and who was undoubtedly a United States official, made a little speech and then read a rather long[Pg 4] paper—the Emancipation Proclamation, I think. After the reading we were told that we were all free and could go where we pleased.

"My mother, who was standing by my side, leaned over and kissed her children, while tears of joy ran down her cheeks. She explained to us what it all meant; that this was the day for which she had so long been praying, but fearing she would never live to see.

"For some minutes," he continues, "there was great rejoicing, and thanksgiving and wild scenes of ecstasy. But there was no feeling of bitterness. In fact, there was pity among the slaves for our former owners. The wild rejoicing of the emancipated colored people lasted but a brief period, for I noticed that by the time they returned to their cabins there was a change in their feelings. The great responsibility of being free, of having charge of themselves and their children, of having to plan for themselves and their children, seemed to take possession of them. To some it seemed, now that they were in actual possession of it, freedom was a more serious thing than they had expected to find. Gradually one by one, stealthily at first, the older slaves began to wander back to the 'big house' to have whispered conversations with their former owners as to their future."

Thus it was that freedom came to Washington and so it came, perhaps, to some three and one-half millions of others on their plantations throughout the South.

Shortly after the "surrender," as the Southern people say, young Washington made a long journey across the mountains with his mother to West Virginia where his stepfather was then living, and it was in Malden he grew up to young manhood. Malden is situated in the mining region of West Virginia, and after a time young Washington went to work in the mines. It was while he was working down in the coal mines of West Virginia[Pg 5] that he one day overheard one of the miners reading from a paper concerning a school at Hampton, Virginia, where a Negro in earnest would be given a chance to work his way through school. He determined at once that he would seek out and find that school. So it was that a few months later he set out afoot across the mountain in the direction of Richmond to find his way to Hampton Institute. In his remarkable biography he has described how he made that journey; how he arrived hungry and penniless in the city of Richmond; how he slept for several nights under the sidewalk in Richmond until he was able to earn enough money to reach the famous school of which he had read.

In this same biography he has told, also, of how the teacher in charge, who was very doubtful about admitting him at first, finally, in place of asking him any questions about what he had learned in school, set him to work sweeping and dusting the schoolroom.

"I swept that recitation room three times," he said, "then I got a dusting cloth and I dusted it four times. All the woodwork around the walls, every bench, table and desk, I went over four times with my dusting cloth. I had the feeling that my future depended upon the way I dusted that room."

When he had finished the teacher came and looked very critically over the results of his work. Then she said: "I guess you will do," and that was his entrance examination. This rather peculiar entrance examination illustrates the spirit of the institution in which Booker Washington gained his first forward preparation for life.

At the time that young Washington entered Hampton Institute, General Armstrong, the founder of the school, was engaged in a great and interesting experiment. His purpose was to create a school which would give the sons of the freedmen education in character as well as in[Pg 6] books. Booker Washington saw that this education was the thing above all others that the masses of the Negro people needed at this time, and realized better than any other of the graduates of the institution the significance and bearing of the work that General Armstrong was trying to do. He made up his mind then that he would go out into some part of the South and establish a school which would do for other members of his race what Hampton had done for him. His opportunity came when a call came to Hampton for a man to take charge of a school at Tuskegee, Alabama. It was thus in 1881 that the famous Tuskegee Institute came to be started.

This school, which was started on July 4, 1881, in a little shanty church, with one teacher and thirty students, has grown until it now has a student body of 1600, with 165 teachers and officers, 103 buildings and property to the value of $1,500,000.

In 1895 Mr. Washington was invited to speak at the Atlanta Cotton States Exposition on Negroes Day. In that speech he made an appeal for peace between the races, and formulated a program for mutual cooperation between black and white which has been the basis of all his efforts since that time.

From that time on his fame has grown steadily, both in this country and abroad. In 1896 Harvard University conferred upon him the honorary degree of Master of Arts for service in the education of his race. He has received numerous other honors since that time and has spoken in every state of the Union in favor of Negro education. A few years ago when he went abroad he was invited to dinner by the King of Denmark. In April, 1912, there was held under his leadership at Tuskegee an international conference on the Negro to which representatives came from many parts of Africa as well as the West Indies and South America. The[Pg 7] result of this was a plan to form a permanent international organization to study the Negro problem in all parts of the world and hold meetings triennially.

Mr. Washington is the author of several books in addition to his autobiography, "Up From Slavery," which has been translated into every civilized language in the world, including Japanese.

The most noted of these books are, "Working with the Hands," "The Story of the Negro," in two volumes, "My Larger Education," and "The Man Farthest Down," which is a record of a journey of observation and study of the working and peasant peoples of Europe.

[Pg 8]

Booker T. Washington

[Pg 9]

The Story of Slavery

I

It was one hot summer's day in the month of August 1619, as the story goes, that a Dutch man-of-war entered the mouth of the James River, in what is now the State of Virginia, and, coming in with the tide, dropped anchor opposite the little settlement of Jamestown. Ships were rare enough to be remembered in that day, even when there was nothing especially remarkable about them, as there was about this one. But this particular ship was so interesting at the time, and so important because of what followed in the wake of its coming, that it has not been forgotten to this day. The reason for this is that it brought the first slaves to the first English settlement in the New World. It is with the coming of these first African slaves to Jamestown that the story of slavery, so far as our own country is concerned, begins.

Although the coming of the first slave ship to what is now the United States is still remembered, the name of the ship and almost everything else concerning the vessel and its strange merchandise has been forgotten. Almost all that is known about it is told in the diary of John Rolfe, who will be remembered as the man who married the Indian girl, Pocahontas. He says, "A Dutch man-of-war that sold us twenty Negars came to Jamestown late in August, 1619." An old record has[Pg 10] preserved some of the names of those first twenty slaves, and from other sources it is known that the ship sailed from Flushing, Holland. But that is almost all that is definitely known about the first slave ship and the first slaves that were brought from Africa to the United States.

The first slaves landed in Virginia were not, by any means, the first slaves that were brought to the New World. Fifty years before Columbus landed on the island of San Salvador, the first African slaves were brought from the West Coast of Africa to Spain, and we know from historical references and records that Negro slavery had become firmly established in Spain before Columbus made his first voyage. It was, therefore, natural enough that the Spanish explorers and adventurers, following close upon the heels of Columbus in search of gold, should bring their Negro servants with them.

It seems likely, from all that we can learn, that a few Negroes were sent out to the West Indies as early as 1501, only eleven years after the discovery of America and one hundred and twenty years before the first cargo of slaves was landed in Jamestown. Four years later, in a letter dated September 15, 1505, written by King Ferdinand to one of his officials in Hispaniola, which we now call Hayti, he says among other things: "I will send you more Negro slaves as you request. I think there be an hundred."

Thus early was Negro slavery introduced into the New World and what do you suppose was the reason, or rather the excuse, for bringing black men to America at this time?

It was to save from slavery the native Indians. A good priest by the name of Las Casas, who accompanied the first Spanish explorers and conquerors, found that the native people, the Indians, were fast dying out under[Pg 11] the cruel tasks put upon them by their Spanish conquerors. Unaccustomed to labor, they could not endure the hardships of working in the mines. The Negroes, on the contrary, had, in many cases, been slaves in their own country, and had been accustomed to labor. At the same time it was said that one Negro could do the work of four Indians. So it was that this good man, out of pity for the enslaved Americans, proposed that the black people of Africa should be brought over to take their places.

Thus the traffic in African slaves began, and in the course of the next three hundred years many millions of black people were carried across the ocean and settled in slave colonies in the New World. They were brought to America, first of all, to work in the mines, and afterwards more of them were brought to do the almost equally difficult pioneer work on the plantations. Thus, in all hard labor of clearing and draining the land, building roads and opening up the New World to cultivation and to civilization, the black man did his part.

It has been estimated that no less than 12,000,000 slaves were transplanted from Africa to America to supply the demand for labor in the West Indies, in South America and in the United

States, during the centuries that the white people of Europe were seeking to establish their civilization in the Western World.

Perhaps as many as 12,000,000 more, who were taken in the wars and raids in Africa, died on the way to the coast, or in the terrible "middle passage," as the journey from the coast of Africa to that of America was called. Many of those captured and sold in Africa, who did not die on the high seas in the crowded and stifling hold of the ships into which they were thrust, did not survive what was known as the "seasoning process," after they were landed in America.

[Pg 12]

Roughly speaking, it is safe to say that not less than 24,000,000 human beings were snatched from their homes in Africa and sold into slavery, to help in building up the world in which we live today in America.

Although African slavery was introduced into America at first in order to save from extinction the native people of the West Indies, who were not strong enough to endure the hardships of slavery, it is sad to recall that the slavery of the Negro did not serve to preserve the Indian, for it was but a comparatively few years after the Spaniards landed in the West Indies before nearly all the native tribes had been swept away. There are today in the West Indies only a few remnants of the Indians whom Columbus met when he first landed in America.

The black man, on the other hand, in spite of the hardships he has endured, has not only survived but has greatly increased in numbers. So greatly has the black man increased that in the West Indies today the black population far outnumbers all other races represented among the inhabitants. Altogether, it is estimated there are now about 24,591,000 Negroes in North and South America and the West Indies. Of this number 10,000,000 are in the United States.

[Pg 13]

II

The story of the first American voyage to Africa to obtain slaves of which there is any definite record, is that of a certain Captain Smith, commanding the ship, Rainbowe, and sailing from Boston. Captain Smith had sailed to Madeira with a cargo of salt fish and staves and, on the way home, he touched on the coast of Guinea for slaves. There happened to be very few slaves for sale at the moment and on this account, Captain Smith, together with the masters of some London slave ships already on the ground, conspired together to pick a quarrel with some of the natives, so as to have an excuse to attack their village and carry off the prisoners made as slaves. Captain Smith's share of the booty was two slaves with whom he returned to Boston.

It happened, however, that when he reached home he got into a quarrel with the ship's owners over the proceeds of the voyage, and, in the lawsuits which resulted, the story of the manner in which the slaves were obtained was told in court. Thereupon one of the magistrates charged Captain Smith with a "threefold offence—murder, man-stealing and Sabboth breaking." He was acquitted of all three charges on the ground that these crimes were committed in Africa, but, as a result of the trial, the slaves were returned to their homes.

This story is interesting, for one reason because it shows that, in the early days of the slave trade, the barter and sale of Negro slaves, so long as it was conducted in an honest and orderly way, according to the[Pg 14] accepted customs and manners of trade, was not considered a wrong or wicked business.

At first the slave traders purchased slaves only from the native chiefs. These slaves were generally prisoners who had been taken in the tribal wars. In some cases they were men or women who had been sold for debt. There were, also, other ways in which one black man in Africa might hold another in slavery.

Very soon, however, the ordinary sources of supply of slaves was not sufficient to meet the demand of the American trade. Then traders became less scrupulous. They began buying from any one who had a man or woman for sale. This encouraged kidnapping. Not infrequently the man who brought a gang of slaves to the coast to be sold would himself be kidnapped and sold by other men before he could return home. Sometimes the traders, after they had purchased a gang or a "coffle" of slaves, as they were called, would invite the traders on board ship in order to entertain them. Then, after they were under the influence of liquor, they would put chains upon them and carry them away with the very slaves the traders themselves a few hours before had sold.

As time went on, and the demand for slave labor increased, the men engaged in this cruel traffic became hardened to its cruelty and the West Coast of Africa became one vast hunting ground. Men and women were tracked and hunted as if they were wild beasts. It grew so bad at length that the conscience of the civilized world was aroused. Then, one by one, the nations of the world began to prohibit the traffic. England, which had formerly been one of the nations most deeply involved in this evil business, now became the leader in the attempt to put a stop to it.

The importation of slaves was prohibited in the United[Pg 15] States in 1808, but that did not put an end to the importation of slaves. For, after the invention of the cotton gin at the close of the eighteenth century by Eli Whitney, a Connecticut school master, slaves were needed more than ever, to plant and till and pick the cotton which had now become much more valuable than before.

Although it was no longer lawful to import slaves, they were smuggled into the country. As late as 1860 the famous yacht, Wanderer, which had at one time been owned by a member of the New York Yacht Club, brought into the United States 450 slaves, and it has been estimated that as many as 15,000 slaves were smuggled into the different Southern ports in the year 1858.

At this time it had become the custom to gather great numbers of slaves at different points along the coast of Africa, in what were called barracoons. These were nothing more or less than strong stockades made by planting trees close together in the ground so as to form a strong enclosure from which there was no escape. In these barracoons slaves captured in the interior were held until they were ready to be shipped.

Swift sailing vessels, which travelled so fast that, once they escaped the vigilance of the war ships stationed along the coast, they could never be overtaken, were used to carry the slaves from the coast of Africa to that of America.

These vessels would hover about in the neighborhood of one of these slave barracoons until the coast was clear; then swiftly the living cargo would be hurried aboard, and the vessel would put on all sail and make all possible haste to put itself and its human freight beyond the reach of the police ships.

Usually these slave ships were provided with a lower, or what was called a "slave deck," beneath the ordinary deck of the ship. In some instances, in order to escape[Pg 16] suspicion, the ship would have no permanent slave deck but such a deck would be hastily arranged after the vessel arrived in the neighborhood of one of the slave barracoons. In such cases the ordinary cargo would be put in the bottom of the ship and then, above this and from three to five feet beneath the ordinary deck, a second deck would be hastily improvised. Here as many slaves would be stowed away as could be possibly crowded into the narrow space.

It is only necessary to read the descriptions of the methods by which this traffic was carried on to understand the horrible suffering to which the slaves were subjected during this middle passage. In many instances, when brought out on deck for a little air, the slaves had to be chained to keep them from jumping overboard.

Sometimes a pestilence would break out on one of these ships and the whole cargo, consisting of three or four hundred slaves, would be lost. It is said that the yellow fever was brought to America by slaves. There are instances, also, where the captain of a slave ship jettisoned, that is to say, threw over-board, a whole ship-load of slaves to escape being caught by the ships that were pursuing him.

When a slave ship reached the shore of America there were snug harbors at various points along the coast into which one of these swift sailing vessels could always hide until its cargo of slaves had been discharged. The island upon which the present city of

Galveston is built was once a refuge for slave pirates and slave smugglers. The coast of Louisiana is full of shallow bays, which reach far into the land, and they were a favorite resort for slave smugglers. Here was the hiding place of the Barataria pirates who were long famous as slave smugglers.

Mobile Bay was one of the points at which a slave[Pg 17] cargo was occasionally landed. It is said that the hull of the very last slave ship, the Lawrence, which was captured and burned by the Federal troops during the first year of the Civil War, may still be seen hidden away in the swamps and marshes east of Mobile.

There is still living in the suburbs of Mobile a little colony of Africans who were brought over on this last slave ship. When they were released by the Federal officers they settled here. It is said that there are old men living in this settlement who still speak an African language, but their children have all grown up to be good Americans.

Once a ship load of slaves was landed on the American coast, they were immediately divided and scattered in every direction. Some were taken to one plantation, others to another, and so on until all were disposed of. Soon they were so thoroughly intermingled with the great body of slaves that all trace of them was lost. At least it was rare that anyone ever did trace the cargo of slaves after it was once landed, although slave ships were frequently captured on the high seas.

When slavers were captured red-handed on the high seas by the United States or English navies, an effort was made to return the slaves to their homes in Africa. As this was not practical the English government established at Sierra Leone, on the west coast of Africa, a station to which they sent all liberated slaves. It was in this manner, that what is now one of the most thriving English colonies on the west coast of Africa was started.

The story of the slave trade is one of the darkest chapters in the history of the Western World, for though it began in the comparatively harmless way already described, it grew steadily worse until in its last stages even those familiar with slavery in its worst form came to look upon it with shame.

[Pg 18]

And yet, in spite of all the suffering that it entailed, and in spite of its degrading effect upon the people who engaged in it, we can see, as we look back upon it now, that some good has come out of it. It served, for one thing, to bring a large number of the savage people of Africa into closer contact with the enlightenment and civilization of the Western World. In the end, it aroused in the minds of some of the best people in Europe and America a new interest in Africa and led hundreds of good Christian people to give up the security of their comfortable homes and give their lives to the task of uplifting and educating the neglected races of the Dark Continent.

Among the first and greatest of those who gave their lives for this purpose was the missionary, David Livingstone, who did more than anyone else to arouse the world to the iniquities of the African slave trade.

[Pg 19]

III

Although, slavery was introduced into Virginia as early as 1619 it was not until nearly one hundred years later that African slaves began to be brought into the English colonies in any very large numbers. For nearly a century the bulk of the rough labor in the field and in the forest was performed, not by Negro slaves, but by white bond servants, who were imported from England and sold like other merchandise in the markets of the colonies.

In 1673, for example, the average price of a bond servant in the colonies, so the historian Bancroft tells us, was ten pounds. At this same time a Negro slave was worth twenty-five pounds.

It was often that the almshouses and prisons of England were emptied in order to furnish laborers for America. It should be remembered, however, that many of the persons who were sent out as bond servants to America were political prisoners, and some of these were persons of quality.

When there was a civil war in England the victorious party frequently disposed of its prisoners by sending them to the colonies as bond servants, or even as slaves. Thousands of Irish Catholics were sent over to America in this way, and it is said that the hardships which these unfortunate bondsmen suffered on the voyage was hardly less than those endured by the African slaves.

It should be remembered, also, in the case of these white bond servants, as in that of the Negro slaves, the sale of human beings began innocently enough. At the[Pg 20] time the English colonies were planted in America there was comparatively little free labor anywhere, and especially was this true of farm labor.

The freedom and independence which seem now to be the natural rights of everyone were enjoyed by very few among the masses of the laboring people in Europe one hundred or two hundred years ago. At that time nearly everyone who worked with his hands was bound, in one way or another, to a master who had control over his actions to an extent which amounted to something like servitude. But it was to the man on the soil and in the country that freedom has everywhere come most slowly. In fact, it was not until the middle of the last century that the complete emancipation of the serfs took place in Western Europe. It was not until 1861, two years before Abraham Lincoln's Emancipation Proclamation set the American Negroes free, that the Russian serfs were emancipated.

It is necessary to remember these facts if we wish to understand how it came about that the slavery of the black man and the servitude of the white man came to be established in this country.

When the first bond servants were sent to America it was not intended that they should be transferred and sold from one owner to another. It was merely intended that they should be bound to labor for the man who paid their passage money until that sum had been repaid. Gradually, however, in their eagerness to obtain labor, people lost sight of the fact that the merchandise they were selling was human beings. It was not long, therefore, before the bond servant was rated among the other property, the horses, the sheep and the cattle, in the inventories of the estate, and he could be disposed of by will and deed along with the remainder of the stock on the plantation.

[Pg 21]

At first the only legal distinction between the bond servant and the Negro slave was that the one was a servant for a period of years and the other was a servant for life. In the long run, however, this distinction made a great difference. In the first place, as the number of these bond servants who became free increased there grew up in the colonies a considerable body of citizens who had known the trials and hardships of servitude. These people naturally sympathized with those of their own class and this created a sentiment against white servitude.

The case of the Negro, however, was different. He was a man of a different race and he was doomed to perpetual servitude. The result was, as time went on, it came to be regarded as the natural vocation and destiny of the man with the black skin to be the servant and the slave of the white man.

One thing that helped to fix the status of the black man, and which finally resulted in the passing away of white servitude in favor of Negro slavery, was the fact that the Negro was better fitted to perform the hard pioneer work which the time demanded. Particularly was this true in the more Southern colonies, like Georgia and the Carolinas.

In South Carolina an effort had been made to reestablish serfdom as it had existed in England one hundred years before. In Georgia, it was at first hoped, by prohibiting slavery to establish a system of free labor. In both instances the effort failed and, after a very few years, Negro slavery was as firmly established in Georgia as it had been in the neighboring state of South Carolina.

Still later, efforts were made to establish white servitude in Louisiana and large numbers of German "redemptioners," as they were called, were brought over[Pg 22] for this purpose. In a very few years these colonists had been swept away by disease.

In one of the reports setting forth "the true state" of the colony of Georgia it was said that, "hardly one-half of the servants of working people were able to do their masters or themselves the least labor: and the yearly sickness of each servant, generally speaking, cost his master as much as would have maintained a Negro for four years."

With the introduction of rice planting the necessity of employing Africans was doubled, because, as it was said, "white servants would have exhausted their strength in clearing a spot for their own graves."

Thus it came about that Negro slavery grew up on the mainland to replace the servitude of the white man, just as it had grown up in the West Indies to take the place of the slavery of the native Indians.

It most not be assumed, however, that the Negro slaves, because they were better able than the white man to stand the hardships of labor in the New World, did not suffer from the effects of the work they were compelled to do. The truth is that so many of them died that the stock of slaves had to be continually replenished. In some parts of the country it was even said of the slave, as one hears it sometimes said of horses, that it paid to work them to death. It was a rule on some of the plantations that the stock of slaves was to be renewed every seven years.

One of the effects of the passing away of white servitude was to make the distance between the free white man and the black slave seem greater than ever. There grew up in the minds of white people, and, to a certain extent, in the minds of black people, the notion that slavery was the natural condition of the Negro just as freedom was the natural condition of the white man.[Pg 23] People began to feel that the black man did not have the same human feelings as the white man; that his pains and his sorrows were somehow not as real and did not have to be considered in the same way that one would consider these same feelings in a white man. All this sentiment of the one race for the other entered into the system of slavery and made it what it became finally before it was abolished as a result of the Civil War.

What this system really was can not be best shown by any account of the cruelties that were sometimes practiced upon slaves, because these cruelties were not practiced by the best masters and were not supported by public sentiment.

The best expression of the innate wrong of slavery will be found in the decision of a Chief Justice of South Carolina in the case of a man who had been tried for beating his slave. In this decision, which affirmed the right of the master to inflict any kind of punishment upon a slave, short of death, it is stated that, in the whole history of slavery there has been no prosecution of a master for punishing his slave.

It had been said in the course of the trial of this case that the relations of the master and slave were like those of parent and child. Justice Ruffin, in delivering the decision, said that this was not so. The object of a parent in training his son, for example, was to fit him to live the life of a free man, and, as a means to that end, he gave him moral and intellectual instruction. There was, said the Justice, no sense in addressing moral instruction to a slave. He said:

"The end is the profit of the master, his security, and the public safety; the subject, one doomed in his own person and his posterity to live without knowledge and without the capacity to make anything his own, and to toil that another may reap the fruit. What moral [Pg 24]consideration shall be addressed to such a being to convince him, what it is impossible but that the most stupid must feel and know can never be true—that he is thus to labor upon a principle of natural duty or for the sake of his own personal happiness. Such services can only be expected from one who has no will of his own, who surrenders his will in implicit obedience to that of another. Such obedience is the consequence only of uncontrolled authority over the body. There is nothing else which can operate to produce the effect. The power of the master must be absolute to render the submission of the slave perfect."

In making this decision Justice Ruffin did not attempt to justify the rule he had laid down on moral grounds. "As a principle of right," he said, "every person must repudiate it, but in the actual condition of things it must be so; there is no remedy. This discipline belongs to the state of slavery. It constitutes the curse of slavery both to the bond and free portion of our population."

Thus it is clear that at the bottom of slavery is the idea that one man's evil is or can be some other man's good.

[Pg 25]

IV

Although there was much of evil connected with slavery, much that tended to weaken the master as well as to injure the slave, there was also a brighter, kindlier side to the life of the slave which is not always understood.

There was, for example, a great deal of difference between the life of a slave on a plantation in Virginia, where master and slaves grew up together as members of one household, and the life of a slave on a similar plantation further South. In either case a large plantation was always a little kingdom in itself, and in this little kingdom the black man and the white man frequently learned to live together on terms of intimacy and friendship such as would scarcely have been possible under other conditions.

On one of these large plantations there were usually several types, or one might almost say castes, among the slaves. There were first of all the house servants, many of whom had grown up from childhood in the "Big House" or mansion of the master. These servants usually became in time very much attached to their masters and their master's children and were often regarded as much a part of the household as any other member of the family. It was to this class that the old servants belonged, of whom so many interesting stories are told, illustrating the devotion of the slaves to their masters.

One of the stories that has been repeated in more than one Southern family relates how the old Southern servant followed his master to war; watched over and cared[Pg 26] for him faithfully during all the hardships of the campaign, and finally, when that master had fallen in battle, carried him back to his home to be buried.

There are many instances, also, of which one does not so often hear, in which the friendship and devotion of the old servants to their master's family continued after the Civil War was over and slavery was abolished. Not infrequently these old slaves continued to work for their masters in freedom much as they had done in slavery. Sometimes when the master's family became poor, the former slave secretly supported them.

There is a story of one man who had agreed before the war broke out to buy his freedom from his master for a certain sum. After freedom came he continued to make the payments just the same until the entire sum was paid, because he knew his master's family was poor and needed the money.

Another class of slaves on the big plantation was composed of the artisans and skilled workmen of every kind, for every one of these large plantations was organized, as nearly as possible, so as to provide for every want of its inhabitants.

Beneath this class of skilled laborers there were the field hands, who did all the common work under the direction of an overseer, sometimes with the help of Negro "drivers."

In addition to all the others there was usually on every large plantation a slave preacher, who might at the same time be a trusted employee of one kind or another. He was at any rate a natural leader among his own people, and often a man of great influence and authority among the slaves, and was frequently a sort of intermediary between them and their master.

The conditions of slavery were harder, as a rule, on the big plantations farther South. These regions were usually peopled by a class of enterprising persons who[Pg 27] had come, perhaps, from Virginia or some of the older slave states. They had removed to the new country in order to find virgin soil, on which large fortunes were made in raising cotton.

In these regions, especially where the slaves were left in charge of an overseer, whose sole function was to make the plantation pay, the slaves came to be treated a great deal more like the mules and the rest of the stock on the plantation. They were treated as if their whole reason for existence consisted in the ability of their owners to use them to make corn, cotton and sugar.

In spite of the bad reputation which the plantations in the far South had among the slaves of Virginia, and in spite of the horror which all the slaves in the border states had of being "sold South," there were many plantations like those of Joseph and Jefferson Davis, the President of the Southern Confederacy and his brother, where the relations between the master and slave were as happy as one could ask or expect, under the circumstances.

The history of the Davis family and of the two great plantations, the "Hurricane" and the "Brierfield," which they owned in Mississippi, is typical. In 1818 Joseph Davis, who was the elder brother of Jefferson, and at that time a young lawyer in Vicksburg, took his father's slaves and went down the river to a place now called Davis' Bend. He was attracted thither by the rich bottom land, which was frequently overflowed by the spring floods of the Mississippi.

At this time there were no steamboats on the Mississippi and the country was wild and lonely. In a few years, with the aid of his slaves, Mr. Davis succeeded in building up a plantation of about 5,000 acres, which soon became known as one of the largest and richest in the whole State of Mississippi, where there were many large and rich plantations.

[Pg 28]

Some years after the settlement at Davis' Bend, Joseph Davis was joined by his brother Jefferson, who lived for several years on the adjoining plantation, known as the "Brierfields."

Joseph Davis had peculiar notions about the government of his slaves. It was a maxim with him that, "the less people are governed, the more submissive they will be to control."

This idea he attempted to carry out in the government of his slaves. Thus he instituted on the plantation a certain measure of self-government. For example, his plantation, like that of his brother Jefferson, was turned over, so far as its agricultural operations were concerned, almost wholly into the hands of one of his slaves. Under the direction of this man the land was surveyed, the levees constructed and the buildings erected. This same man was allowed to conduct a store of his own. He bought and sold goods, not only among the hands on the plantation, but among the hands on other plantations. Sometimes Mr. Davis himself was several hundred dollars in debt to him for goods purchased.

Mr. Davis also instituted a jury system for the trial of minor offences committed by his slaves. In a court thus constituted a jury of slaves passed judgment on their fellows, Mr. Davis reserving for himself, however, the pardoning power. When a slave could do better for himself at some other form of work than day labor he was allowed the liberty to do so, giving in money, or other equivalent, the worth of ordinary service in the field. There was at one time a school on the plantation, taught by a poor white man, in which the white children from the Big House as well as some of the children of the more favorite slaves went to school together.

In this novel and statesman-like way Joseph Davis sought to carry out his notion of making the plantation,[Pg 29] as near as possible under the circumstances, a little self-governing community. After freedom came it was Joseph Davis' plan to keep all his former slaves on the plantation and, as they grew in intelligence and ability to care for themselves, to make them its owners. To this end he sold the plantation to the man who had been his overseer. This man, with his two sons, all of whom had formerly been slaves on the plantation, continued for a number of years to carry on the work of the plantation until, as the result of losses, due to overflow, it became apparent they would not be able to pay the heavy interest charges which the purchase of the place had entailed and were thus forced to give up the experiment.

It is a mistake to assume that life for the slave on the plantation was always one of unremitting labor. In a humble way the slaves had their seasons of rejoicing and festivity. There were the usual weekly meetings in the plantation churches, where they had sermons, sometimes by a white minister, but more often by one of their own number. It was here that those beautiful old plantation melodies sprang up, in which the slaves poured out, in rude but picturesque language and in simple plaintive melodies, what lay deepest and heaviest on their hearts.

Sometimes at night, around the fireside, they listened to those quaint and homely stories which have been preserved in classic form in the Tales of Uncle Remus.

"Hog-killing" was a sort of annual festival among the slaves, and the occasional cornshuckings were always a joyous event in which both master and servants, each in their separate ways, took part.

These cornshucking bees took place during the last of November or the first of December, and were a sort of prelude to the festivities of the Christmas season. After all the corn had been gathered it would be piled[Pg 30] up in the shape of a great mound. Then invitations would be sent around by the master of one of the large plantations to the neighboring plantations, inviting them and their slaves to be present on a certain night. In response to these invitations as many as one or two hundred men, women and children would come together.

After all were assembled around the pile of corn some one, who had already gained a reputation as a leader in singing, would climb on top of the mound and begin at once, in a clear loud voice, to sing. He sang a song of the cornshucking season, making up the words very largely as he went along. All the others gathered at the base of the mound and joined of course in the chorus. The whole proceeding had a good deal of the flavor of the campmeeting and some of the music was weird and wild.

One of the songs that used to be sung on occasions like this ran about as follows:

Massa's niggers am slick and fat,
Oh! Oh! Oh!
Shine just like a new beaver hat,
Oh! Oh! Oh!

Refrain:—

Turn out here and shuck dis corn,
Oh! Oh! Oh!
Biggest pile o' corn seen since I was born,
Oh! Oh! Oh!
Jones's niggers am lean an' po';
Oh! Oh! Oh!
Don't know whether dey get 'nough to eat or no,
Oh! Oh! Oh!

[Pg 31]

Refrain:—

Turn out here and shuck dis corn;
Oh! Oh! Oh!
Biggest pile o' corn seen since I was born,
Oh! Oh! Oh!

Half the charm of Southern life was made by the presence of the Negro. The homes that had no Negro servants were dreary by contrast with those that did.

The native quality of the Negro, his natural sympathy, cheerfulness and good humor, and above all his fidelity to his master and his master's children, helped to make slavery, for both white man and black man, a very much more tolerable institution than it would otherwise have been.

Almost all that has been said of slavery, whether good or bad, is probably true as far as it goes. The institution had its heartless and its human side, and, since slavery is no more, it is perhaps better to close this story with this brighter and more cheerful view.

www.ingramcontent.com/pod-product-compliance
Lightning Source LLC
Chambersburg PA
CBHW071345290326
41933CB00040B/2351